THE DRAWER BOY

Michael Healey

Playwrights Canada Press
Toronto • Ontario

Playwrights Canada Press
215 Spadine Ave, Suite 230 Toronto, Ontario CANADA M5T 2C7
416-703-0013   fax 416-703-0059
orders@playwrightscanada.com • www.playwrightscanada.com

Playwrights Canada Press acknowledges the support of
the taxpayers of Canada and the province of Ontario through
The Canada Council for the Arts and the Ontario Arts Council.

Art & Soul. Cover photograph by Howard Chang.   *Cover design by*

Canadian Cataloguing in Publication Data

Healey, Michael
    The drawer boy
A play
ISBN: 0-88754-568-8

I. Theatre Passe Muraille. Farm show. I. Title.

PS8565.E14D62 1999a   C812'.54   C99-931193-X
PR9199.3.H42D62 1999a

First edition: May 1999. Second printing: November 1999. Third revised
printing, January 2001. Fourth printing: December 2001. Fifth printing:
August 2002. Seventh printing: April 2004.

Printed and bound by AGMV Marquis at Quebec, Canada.

for my parents

Actor and writer Michael Healey's first play, *Kicked*, was nominated for a Chalmers Award and won a Dora for Best New Play (1998). He has toured the show throughout Canada and internationally. He has also written two chapbooks about the theatre: *Dear Mr Newton, Sincerely Michael Healey*, and *An Actor's Diary*. *The Drawer Boy* is his second play.

PRODUCTION HISTORY

The Drawer Boy premiered at Toronto's Theatre Passe Muraille on February 25, 1999, with the following cast and crew:

MORGAN	Jerry Franken
ANGUS	David Fox
MILES	Tom Barnett
Director	Miles Potter
Set Design	Stephan Droege
Lighting Design	Steve Lucas
Costume Design	Michelle Vanderheyden
Sound Design	Jonathan Rooke
Stage Manager	Erica Heyland
Production Manager	Mark Ryder
Technical Director	Jonathan Rooke

PLAYWRIGHT'S NOTES

Gerard Manley Hopkins' poem "At The Wedding March" is quoted in Act Two.

Miles Potter's input at every stage of this play's growth was invaluable. My thanks also to the actors who participated in workshops: Tom Hauff, Gary Rieneke, Raoul Bhaneja, David Fox, Jordan Pettle, Eric Peterson, Jerry Franken, and Tom Barnett. I'm grateful to Ted Johns for his enthusiasm and generosity; to Janet Amos and the Blyth Festival for providing the original impetus; and to Iris Turcott and Brian Quirt for their notes. Thanks to Neil Foster and Factory Theatre, to Kim McCaw and the Banff Playwright's Colony, and to the Toronto and Ontario Arts Councils. Kate Lynch's advice was always helpful and, more importantly, beautifully timed. Plus, she gave me the Hopkins. Thanks as well to Barbara Gordon, Mark Ryder, Allegra Fulton, Steve Lucas, David Kinsman, and Jacoba Knaapen.

Special thanks to Don and Alison Lobb, who fed me dinner and talked about *The Farm Show* like it happened last weekend.

CHARACTERS

MORGAN, in his fifties

ANGUS, also in his fifties

MILES, in his twenties

ACT ONE

ACT 1, SCENE 1

The kitchen of a central Ontario farm house, in the summer of 1972. It is dominated by a large, old oak table; there is a wood stove for heat and a rather modern oven in some ghastly colour. The decorating touches are either from the forties, or are non-existent. There is a back door stage-left, with a small, unheated mud room. Downstage is a yard (with chickens? small vegetable garden?), and off stage-right is the barn.

Lights up. ANGUS is alone in the kitchen. There is a long moment where he sits, then eventually gets up and starts making sandwiches. Just as he finishes one, MORGAN comes into the kitchen.

ANGUS   Morgan! Hello!

MORGAN takes the sandwich, eats a couple of bites, and then leaves, taking the sandwich. ANGUS starts to make another sandwich. Meanwhile, MILES wanders into the yard. He looks at the farmhouse, leaves, then comes back and knocks on the door. ANGUS opens the door.

ANGUS   Hello!

MILES   Good morning, sir. My name's—

ANGUS   Hey! Who're you?

MILES   I'm.... My name's Miles.

ANGUS   Miles! Hello!

MILES   Hi. I'm from Toronto.

ANGUS   Oh. That's too bad.

MILES   Yes. Uh, I'm here with a group of actors. We're making up a play about farmers.

ANGUS	Oh.
MILES	Yes. I was wondering—could I help out here in any way? We want to spend time with—
ANGUS	We're farmers.
MILES	I.... Yes. Could you use some help around the farm for the next couple of weeks? Free of charge. I just need a place to stay and the chance to watch you.
ANGUS	Watch me.
MILES	Uh, yes.
ANGUS	Watch me what?
MILES	Well, whatever you do all day. As a farmer.
ANGUS	As a farmer.
MILES	Yes.
ANGUS	I better ask Morgan.
MILES	Okay.
ANGUS	Okay.

> ANGUS *goes inside.* MILES *waits.* ANGUS *heads across the room. He notices the sandwiches and this stops him. He returns to the counter and continues making sandwiches. As he finishes one,* MORGAN *comes in and takes it.*

ANGUS	Morgan! Hello!
MORGAN	Angus. Did I hear you talking?
ANGUS	Talking?
MORGAN	Forget it. Thanks.

> MORGAN *goes.* ANGUS *makes a sandwich and starts to eat.* MILES *waits patiently outside. Slow fade out of lights, as* ANGUS *eats and* MILES *waits.*

Act 1, Scene 2

> *In the blackout, there is noise off right: a tractor engine being gunned. The following dialogue should be only partially audible over the tractor.*

MORGAN   Alright, now. Alright. Give 'er. Little more... little more.

ANGUS   Give 'er. Give 'er. Give 'er.

MILES   Okay....

MORGAN   You got to line up those parts—

MILES   Right.

MORGAN   —so I can connect them.

ANGUS   Give 'er. Give 'er. Give'er.

MORGAN   That's it, son. That's it. Now back it up into place. You want it to go left, so turn the wheel right, yeah? Back it up. Reverse! REVERSE!

MILES   Right on, okay. How do I—where's the— *(the gears grind terribly)* Oh, shit.

ANGUS   Give 'er. GIVE 'ER! GIVE 'ER!

MILES   Alright. I got it. I got it. Okay! *(the motor dies; there's a pause)* Wow. Sorry.

ANGUS   Uh oh. Oh, shit.

MORGAN   Alright, son. Just—start 'er up again.

> *He starts the engine up again.*

MORGAN   Now. Just back it up slow. Just a few feet's all. Just a few more....

ANGUS   Give 'er!

MILES   Oooookay. Ooooooookaaaaaay....

Suddenly the engine roars, then dies. After the briefest of pauses, the following occurs all at once.

MORGAN Eeeezuz Rice! Sonnova...! Arrrgh!

MILES Oh, no. Oh, Jesus.

ANGUS Oh boy. Oh boy, Morgan. OH BOY. Morgan?

MILES Are you okay? Sir? Are you—?

MORGAN Goddamn it.

ANGUS Oh boy, oh boy, oh boy. Oh my.

Lights have come up by now. ANGUS runs on, and into the kitchen; as soon as he gets there, he forgets why. MORGAN enters, sits on the stoop, examining his wounded arm. MILES comes in, writing in a small notebook.

MORGAN Farm's a dangerous place. Put that in yer... play.

MILES You okay?

MORGAN Eyuh.

MILES *(writing)* I'm really, really sorry.

MORGAN Thought you said you knew how to drive a tractor.

MILES Just a sec. *(finishes writing)* I really, really thought I did.

ANGUS wanders out to the stoop and sees MORGAN.

ANGUS Christ! Morgan! What happened to you?

MORGAN Angus. You were there! He backed the tractor over me.

ANGUS Who did?

MORGAN He did.

ANGUS *(noticing MILES)* Hello!

MILES	Hi.
ANGUS	Morgan. Who's that?
MORGAN	Angus. Get me a wet towel, will yeh?
ANGUS	Sure.

> ANGUS *goes inside, to the sink. He pauses, and during the following gets a tablespoon out of a drawer, puts water in it from the tap, and carefully walks it out to the stoop.*

MILES	There's no little "R" on your knob.
MORGAN	'Scuse me?
MILES	And your clutch goes, I think, abnormally far in. I think I should probably not do anything but watch you guys from now on, and take notes. If I just do that, rather than actually help you guys around the farm, I think it'd be better for everyone.
MORGAN	If you want to stay here, you'll help out. Don't mind you being here and doing your playwriting, but I can't see having a pair of hands around here that don't do nothing.
MILES	Alright, I guess I could....

> ANGUS *comes out with the spoonful of water.*

ANGUS	Morgan. Here.

> ANGUS *shoves the spoon in* MORGAN's *mouth.*

MORGAN	Thanks. A towel?
ANGUS	You bet.

> ANGUS *goes back indoors.*

MILES	I think I might be better off if I stick to the animals. Animals like me.
MORGAN	Uh huh.

MILES	Could you tell me about the milking operation?
MORGAN	Cows are milked twice a day, milk goes to the dairy, dairy gives us money.
MILES	Okay, but what's it like? Do the cows mind being milked continually?
MORGAN	Do they mind?
MILES	Yeah, well, you know—how does a cow feel about getting interfered with twice a day?

ANGUS *returns with another spoonful of water.*

MORGAN	*(to* ANGUS*)* Thanks. A towel?
ANGUS	You bet.

ANGUS *goes back inside, and gets another spoonful of water.*

MORGAN	How does the cow feel. About getting milked.
MILES	Yeah. Do they find it traumatic at all?
MORGAN	Well, even though you're from the city, you must know that your cow is the laziest of God's creatures.
MILES	Right.
MORGAN	And I'm sure you realize that we slaughter some of the cows we got. For eatin'.
MILES	Right.
MORGAN	'Bout one a week we slaughter. Keeps the deep freeze full. Maybe you can help with the next one. Well, the way we choose which cow to kill for meat is related to their milk output. Lowest producer gets the axe. The cows know this, and they produce as much milk as they can, to keep from—you know—being chosen.
MILES	I see.

MORGAN	Otherwise, the dang things would stand around all day.
MILES	Really.
MORGAN	Here's what I suggest you do. Go into the barn, sit down with the cows. At first, they'll seem real casual. But just watch them for a while, and before long you'll see just how much pressure they're labouring under. They're all tense as cats.
MILES	Right. Okay! Thanks. *(he starts to leave, then comes back)* Morgan? I'm sorry I hit you with the tractor.
MORGAN	Think nothing of it. Hardly a day goes by on most farms when something or somebody doesn't get run over. I expect you'll find that out firsthand.
MILES	Thanks.

> MILES *exits.* ANGUS *returns with the water, and shoves the spoon in* MORGAN's *mouth.*

MORGAN	Thanks. A towel?
ANGUS	Morgan, I'm tired.
MORGAN	Okay.
ANGUS	Morgan? What happened. I smell bread. Oh boy.

> MORGAN *goes to* ANGUS *and feels his head.*

MORGAN	Okay, Angus. Get upstairs and get to bed. I'll come up and close the curtains. Go now.
ANGUS	Okay. Oh my. The smell... I wonder, I wish... I....
MORGAN	Angus? Upstairs now.

Act 1, Scene 3

Later. MORGAN *is in the kitchen, making a sandwich.* MILES *wanders into the yard. He is staring at his notebook, talking softly.*

MILES

Mooo. Mooo—low. Loooow. Lowing. Loooow. Soooooo. Sooooo scared. Don't want to get eaaaten. Muuuust maaaake miiiilk.

MILES practises bovine look and movements. Satisfied, he makes a final notation and goes into the house.

Morgan. You were right. All those cows are absolutely terrified.

MORGAN

Sandwich?

MILES

Sure. What kind?

MORGAN

Spleen. Beef Spleen.

MILES

Sure. Great. A small one. How's your hand?

MORGAN

Numb. Some of the nerves are crushed, I expect.

MILES

Oh, my God....

MORGAN

Well, at least the throbbing's stopped. If it's not right in a week or so, I'll get it removed.

MILES

You'll...?

MORGAN

Government'll pay for a hook or something. How'er things in the barn?

MILES

Uhh, well, I sat there for a long time, watching your cows. One of them, a brown one—

MORGAN

Which brown one?

MILES

Uh....

MORGAN

Bow-legged brown one, or the brown one that smells like vanilla beans?

MILES   The bow-legged one. I guess.

MORGAN   Daisy.

MILES   She kept trying to turn around to look at me. I think she thought I was coming to choose the next one to get—you know. She looked me in the eye, she—Daisy has these eyes that are like brown tennis balls. She stared and stared right at me. For a long time. It felt like we... exchanged something. Daisy's not... next, is she?

> MORGAN *comes to the table with the sandwiches.*

MORGAN   'Fraid so.

MILES   Jeez. *(eating)* You said this was beef? Tastes like ham.

MORGAN   That's because we feed the pigs to the cows.

MILES   Really?

MORGAN   Well, not the whole pig.

MILES   *(takes notebook out)* What's it like, being around death and rebirth all the time? To grow things and kill things for a living, year in and year out? You've been here how long?

MORGAN   We bought the place in '42.

MILES   So, for thirty years you've been doing this. Planting, nurturing, nourishing, building up; then harvesting, reaping, destroying, eviscerating.

MORGAN   Uh huh.

MILES   Must be... difficult. I mean, you grow wheat and corn out of the dirt, out of literally nothing, then you cut it down and sell it. You raise animals, feed them and house them for years, name them; and then you kill them and eat them.

MORGAN   Uh huh.

MILES	What is that like? How does that make you feel?
MORGAN	Miles, it's an emotional rollercoaster.
MILES	I bet. Is Angus going to have lunch?
MORGAN	Angus is upstairs asleep. He's got one of his headaches.
MILES	Is there something wrong with him? I mean, apart from his being....
MORGAN	Being what?
MILES	Well, uh, you know....
MORGAN	Simple?
MILES	Yeah, I guess.
MORGAN	'The hell do you mean by that?
MILES	Uuuuhh....
MORGAN	He gets headaches. Says he sees lights flashing, sometimes he smells bread baking. Lasts for a day, then he's fine. Sometimes, just before a headache comes on, he'll get giddy. Excited. Then I know to put him to bed.
MILES	Was he always like this?
MORGAN	Angus got knocked down by the front door of a house, in London in '41, during the bombing. He's got a plate in his skull that keeps the two broken parts of it from rubbing together. Before that, he was just like you or me. We went over together, and came back together. We grew up.
MILES	And you've taken care of him since the war?
MORGAN	He doesn't need much taking care of. Angus's no invalid. I show him how to do things, remind him. He can run the tractor, he can use the stove. Knits. Does the accounts. You should see him with a bunch of figures. Only thing that makes Angus different is he can't remember from one minute to the next. He only knows right now. He won't remember you.

MILES	Ever?
MORGAN	Nope. You'll have to tell him who you are, what you're doing here, probably every morning.
MILES	What do the doctors say?
MORGAN	They say he's normal, for someone who's had done to him what he's had.
MILES	Will he ever—I mean, is he....
MORGAN	Angus's fine. He stays here, does what I've taught him—we're just fine.
MILES	You've lived here alone since the war?
MORGAN	Yup. We bought this land right after. Finish up. Plenty to do this afternoon.
MILES	*(wolfing sandwich and rising)* Right. Nothing dangerous, I hope.
MORGAN	Nah. Ever gutted anything?
MILES	You mean—what—like, cut the guts out of something?
MORGAN	Uh huh. Do you know how to use a chainsaw?
MILES	I, uhh. *(remembers the tractor)* No. No sir, I don't.
MORGAN	Nothing to it. Just put on the welder's mask and the raincoat, and hold on tight when things get slippery.
MILES	Think it's a good idea? After the tractor?
MORGAN	Probably not. But there'll be no mollycoddling on this farm while there's work to do. Plus, I'll stand well back.
MILES	They're not going to believe this at rehearsal.
	ANGUS *enters, disoriented and in pain. The light hurts him. He's looking for something.*
ANGUS	Morgan? Hello. The car got scratched. Right?

MORGAN	You need to be lying down. You know, Angus.
ANGUS	Right. *(pointing to MILES)* Who'r... you?
MILES	My name's Miles. I'm staying here with you while I put on a play about farmers.
ANGUS	Tall. You look like... standing there, beside the... the girl.
MORGAN	*(to MILES)* You go ahead, meet you in the barn.
MILES	Sure.

MILES *exits.*

MORGAN	Angus. Come now. Come up.
ANGUS	*(softly, as MORGAN leads him out)* You bet.

ACT 1, SCENE 4

Lights up. ANGUS enters the kitchen. He's look-ing for something, and begins his search by examining a wall. Eventually he starts to look around, opening cupboard doors and looking under things. He's on his hands and knees when MILES limps into the farm house, his hands and thighs raw from moving hay bales. He has some trouble getting the door open.

MILES	Wow. Ow, Jeez.
ANGUS	Hullo. Hey. Get outta here.
MILES	Hello, Angus. My name is Miles and I'm staying with you and Morgan to learn about farming so I can write a play about it.
ANGUS	*(throws a hand up in the air)* Hello, Miles. Okay.

MILES *limps to the sink, starts to tend to his wounds.*

ANGUS	Are yuh hurt? Yuh want some Freshie?
MILES	I was just out helping Morgan with the hay bales. I musta hauled six hundred of the damn things off the wagon and on to the... escalator thing....
ANGUS	The what?
MILES	The—you know—the thing that takes the bales up to the top of the barn.
ANGUS	Oh yeah, that thing's called the... uh.

> ANGUS *goes to the sink during the following, gets* MILES *a spoonful of water.*

MILES	The only way to do that's to drag them off the wagon and sorta throw the bale onto the escalator using your leg. Look at my leg.
ANGUS	It's called the, uh....
MILES	Morgan looks at me and says: "Folks wear long pants around a farm." I bet this is infected. (ANGUS *shoves the water into* MILES' *mouth)* Thanks.
ANGUS	Uh huh. Help yourself.
MILES	Then I go up into the barn to stack the bales, and that's even worse, 'cause there's no air up there—lots of dust, but no air—and I have to pick the damn things up, lift them over my head, and pile them up.
ANGUS	Hey. We got Freshie.
MILES	I wrestled in high school. I've done hard things, Angus. I was a hedgehog in a show last year about a group of dead animals. That show was three hours long. *I didn't move.* I've done hard things. And I wasn't about to quit, not with Morgan watching. I just picked them up, *(demonstrating)* one by one, hauled them over to the side of the barn, built a wall of hay. Look at my hands. Splinters inside of exploded blisters. "The twine, city boy, pick them up by the twine!" For God's sake. I'm not supposed to be doing this. I'm supposed to be writing a play.

ANGUS   Was it hay or straw you were loadin'?

MILES   I dunno. What's the difference?

ANGUS   Between hay and straw?

MILES   Yeah.

ANGUS   Hmmmmm. Nope. Don't know. Wouldn't eat no straw, though.

MILES   Do you think that Morgan's still upset with me over the thing with the tractor?

ANGUS   Thing with the...?

MILES   Running him over with the tractor. I ran him down two mornings ago, remember?

ANGUS   Uuuhhhh. Nope. Tractor, eh?

MILES   Yes. Never mind.

ANGUS   Someone got hit by the tractor?

MILES   Yes, it's okay, Angus. Forget it.

ANGUS   You bet.

MILES   *(points to fridge)* Angus, what's that called?

ANGUS   That's the uuuhhh. Nope.

MILES   Is that the refrigerator?

ANGUS   Sure it is.

MILES   Or the stove?

ANGUS   Morgan. We better ask Morgan that.

MILES   It's okay. *(points to table)* That's the chair, right?

ANGUS   Chair.

MILES   Angus. What's my name?

ANGUS   Don't you know?

MILES	Do you?
ANGUS	Ha ha.
MILES	Okay.
ANGUS	Okay then.
MILES	My name's Miles.
ANGUS	Hello, Miles, okay.
MILES	Angus? Twelve, fifty-six, one-oh-seven, twelve again, and six seventy-nine.
ANGUS	Uh huh.
MILES	What's my name?
ANGUS	Oh. Uuuuhhh. Ha ha.
MILES	Okay, Angus. What about those numbers I said. Can you add them up?
ANGUS	Eight hundred, sixty-six.
MILES	Right! I think that's right....
ANGUS	Oh, yes.
MILES	How old are you?
ANGUS	'Bout your age.
MILES	Oh yeah? Is Morgan our age, too?
ANGUS	Naw. He's an old feller.
MILES	Did you ever fight in the war?
ANGUS	Yes, I did. Sure. Prince's Pats. Went to France, went to England. With Morgan.
MILES	What did you have for breakfast this morning?
ANGUS	Ha ha. Sure.
MILES	And what's my name?

ANGUS *looks at* MILES. *This is starting to upset him.*

MILES   My name's Miles. Angus. Tell me about your head.

ANGUS   Hurts... sometimes... always....

MILES   How'd you hurt it? Do you know?

ANGUS   Morgan says... they were waiting for... hey. What's your name?

MILES   You tell me.

ANGUS   Don't know. Didn't tell me.

MILES   Angus—

ANGUS   Me too! My name's Angus too! Ha ha ha!

MILES   No, Angus. Listen. Your head. In London, did you get hit by a—

ANGUS   Noo, no. No.

MILES   In the bombing—by a, a front door.

ANGUS   Front...? No no no no. I did not.

MILES   Is that what happened, or do you just not remember? Morgan said.

ANGUS   Morgan knows. He knows. He tells me. I... the drawer boy. The tall girls. You see... Morgan... he knows. He knows. He... oh boy. (ANGUS *holds his head and starts to weep*) Ohhh boy....

MILES   Angus. What is it? Are you— (*runs to the door*) Morgan! Morgan! Come quick! Angus, I'm sorry.... Morgan!

MORGAN *enters.*

MORGAN   Jesus. Alright now, Angus. Alright.

MORGAN *goes to the sink and gets a table-spoon of water.*

ANGUS   Morgan? Hello. How did I get hurt?

               MORGAN *shoves the spoon into* ANGUS'
               mouth. ANGUS *calms down somewhat.*

               Thanks. Okay. But.

MORGAN   Hush now.

ANGUS   Was it the front door? Was it?

MORGAN   Hush.

ANGUS   He says....

MORGAN   (*suddenly*) Angus! Make me a sandwich.

ANGUS   Eyuh.

               ANGUS *gets up, goes to the fridge, and gets out*
               sandwich materials. He is almost instantaneously
               distracted by this task, and stops crying.

MORGAN   'The hell have you been doing?

MILES   I didn't mean to upset him. I asked him a few
               questions about the war. His accident....

MORGAN   I thought you were here to find out *about farming.*

MILES   Yes, I—

MORGAN   You don't know what you're doing, asking him
               about that. I told you, his memory's faulty. You
               upset him, he spends the day in bed, and I have
               to do everything by myself. You got questions,
               ask me. I said I'd tell you everything you need to
               know about farming. Stick to the cows and the
               chickens. If you can't do that, you'd better leave.
               Can you do that?

MILES   Yes.

MORGAN   Miles? You better.

MILES   Yes, sir. I'm sorry. (*to* ANGUS) Angus? I'm sorry
               I... I'm sorry about what just happened.

> ANGUS *has no idea what* MILES *is talking about.*

ANGUS Oh. Well, uh... no, no. That's fine. Hey! Who wants Freshie?

ACT 1, SCENE 5

> *Night.* MILES *and* MORGAN *are seated at the table. Dinner is over.* ANGUS *has finished washing up and starts to make bread. He gets out the ingredients and makes dough throughout the scene.* MILES *makes notes furiously through the following.*

MORGAN *(to* MILES*)* You know what a steak costs? Per pound?

ANGUS Dollar forty-seven.

MILES Dollar forty-seven?

MORGAN One dollar forty-seven cents. People scream over a price like that. Drop down dead in the meat aisle when they see that price, but let me tell you something: if the price of that steak had increased in the last ten years as much as the price of a postage stamp, that steak would be a dollar fifty-seven per pound.

ANGUS Eight point oh-two percent.

MORGAN If that steak had gone up like the price of a newspaper, it'd cost a dollar seventy-five.

ANGUS Ten point three percent.

MILES Per pound.

MORGAN Per pound. If that pound of steak had gone up like wages have in the last ten years, it'd cost two-oh-eight a pound.

ANGUS Thirty-nine percent.

MORGAN   And if it'd gone up like the income tax has, that steak would be three-eighty a pound.

ANGUS   Fifty-eight point three three three three three. Percent.

MORGAN   And wouldn't that make people scream blue murder in the grocery store. We get nothing for what we do. An egg costs nine cents in the store, there's practically an armed uprising in the city over how expensive an egg is. Know how much it costs me to produce that egg? Nine point one three cents. Care to guess what my profit margin is on that egg?

ANGUS   Negative eighteen point seven-two cents per gross of eggs.

MORGAN   And if I drop one or two, it gets even worse.

MILES   How can you afford to run a losing business, year in, year out?

MORGAN   I make a little on the milk, and that almost evens things out with the eggs. The rest of the debt I put over to next year, until the year when my crops finally go for what they're actually worth. That year, of course, will never come. Government gets wind of that, they'll start doin' business that way. Then, God help us all.

Public complains about us, they believe all us farmers are making a killing. Politicians complain about us, tired of giving us subsidies that just get us to next year—maybe. Kids are leaving the farms, moving to Toronto; nobody wants to do this anymore. Soon nobody will.

ANGUS   Morgan? Why're you shouting?

MORGAN   Farms in a strip from Windsor to Montreal provide forty percent of the food for the country, and soon they'll all just stop. You'll get your food imported from God knows where, then see how much a pound of steak goes for. You go to university?

MILES   Yeah.

MORGAN   What'd you study?

MILES   English and drama. And political science, and geology, and law, and French. Phys Ed and a little Latin.

MORGAN   Uh huh. Graduate?

MILES   Well, I was living at this place called Rochdale College, and we really didn't believe that the point was to graduate; we thought that we should be able to—

MORGAN   How big a student-loan debt didja run up?

MILES   That's a little personal, Morgan, I—

MORGAN   More that two thousand dollars?

MILES   Oh, yeah.

MORGAN   More than three?

MILES   Well, I sort of missed a term in there—a whole year, really, once the customs thing got cleared up—never mind—so, actually I went for five years, on and off. So it wound up being around thirty-six hundred dollars. All together.

MORGAN   The government gave you more than I paid myself for the last four years.

ANGUS   1968: eight sixty-one. 1969: nine hundred and five. 1970: seven hundred, seventy-four. And 1971: seven hundred and ninety.

MORGAN   Don't you write that down. I make about the same as everyone else out here, but nobody needs to hear the exact figures from your stage.

MILES   Can I use the figures about the pound of steak?

MORGAN   Wish you would.

MILES   This is going to blow peoples' minds in rehearsal. You know, we all just go to the store, buy some fruit or a steak, and never think about where it comes from. Did you ever think of starting up a communal farm?

MORGAN   Eh?

MILES   Have you ever studied the Soviet model? They've been farming communally for decades in Russia, and the results are incredible.

ANGUS   Goddamn communists.

MILES   Productivity is up, the people all have enough to eat, money's not a—

ANGUS   *Goddamn communists.*

MILES   —worry. Anybody who looks at it sees it's the wave of the future. Who are your neighbours to the north?

MORGAN   Lobbs. Don and Alison Lobb.

MILES   What if the fence came down between your two places. What if you and the Lobbs agreed—

ANGUS   *Goddamn communists.*

MILES   —agreed that from now on you'd both work the fields, take turns, maybe even sell one of the tractors—you'd only need the one, one barn for all the animals, an equal division of labour, materials, and profits—

ANGUS   GOD. DAMN. COMMUNISTS!

MORGAN   Angus! Why're *you* shouting?

ANGUS   Was I?

MORGAN   How's that bread coming?

ANGUS *puts the bread in the oven.*

ANGUS   Done!

During the following, ANGUS *goes outside and stands in the yard. He stares up at the stars and becomes transfixed.*

MORGAN   Good. Miles. Let me ask you a question. Now, your answer to this question may have a direct bearing on where you sleep tonight, on how comfortable a place it is you're sleeping in. A place where the humans normally sleep, or a place where furred and feathered animals generally lay their heads. A place that smells a bit. Miles? How would you describe yourself, politically?

MILES   *(after a pause)* Oh. Well, I'm an actor. We don't have politics.

MORGAN   I think that's best. Angus. Don't you let that bread burn.

ANGUS   Bread?

MORGAN   He's ruined more bread.... Where will you be putting on this play of yours?

MILES   Ray Bird is lending us his barn for the first show. Eventually, we hope to do it all over the county. Hope you'll come and see it, both of you. In fact, we're inviting some people to a rehearsal day after tomorrow, just so they can tell us if we're on the right track. Maybe you'd come to that?

MORGAN   Prob'ly will, seeing as how you're going to give your rendition of our cow Daisy.

MILES   Well, maybe not. I did the monologue for the others in the show—you know, "Have to make milk, don't want to get eaten" —and nobody believed it. I couldn't convince anybody that cows are petrified all the time. They want to do the stereotypical cow—you know, placid, dumb, cud-chewing. Bourgeois theatrical cow; that cow that we've seen onstage for years and years. And which of course I now know is a lie. I said, if you want to do a scene about a cow that's a lie, we could have stayed in Toronto and made it up out of our heads. I said I wasn't going to insult Daisy by portraying her without exploring her pain, her anxiety. Her reality. The director said okay, fair enough. And then he cut the scene.

MORGAN   Tough break.

MILES	Yeah. So far they aren't using anything I've brought to rehearsal. Remember the day we piled up all those hay bales? I made up a dance, the dance of the hay-bale stacker. It got cut too.
MORGAN	*(to MILES)* Lemme ask you something. *(goes to the door)* Lie down, Angus.
ANGUS	Morgan. Hello.
MORGAN	Lie down if you want to look at them stars. You'll hurt your neck again.
ANGUS	Okay, Sure.

ANGUS *lies down.*

MORGAN	*(to MILES)* What happens if none of the... things you make up get put in the show?
MILES	Jeez. I don't know. I guess they'd probably have to kick me out of the collective.
MORGAN	So, if you don't produce, you die—is that it?
MILES	...I guess so.
MORGAN	Well, there you go. You have something in common with my cows there.
MILES	You're right.
MORGAN	You got that in common with me, too. I don't produce, I go as sure as you or the cows do.
MILES	Right on. That's good. Mind if I use that?
MORGAN	Guess not.
MILES	Thanks. Think I'll take this upstairs and try to put it into some kind of shape for rehearsal tomorrow.
MORGAN	Right. You'd better get some sleep. We're rotating the crops tomorrow.
MILES	Is that right? That a big job?

MORGAN	Uh huh. We have to dig up all the hay growing on the east side of the field, the hay that gets all the morning sun, and move it to the west side, to get the afternoon sun. Big job. And we have to do it in the dark. Set your alarm for three.
MILES	Three? A.M.??
MORGAN	That's right. And I don't want to have to call you.
MILES	I'll be ready.
MORGAN	See that you are.
MILES	Yes, sir.

> MILES *exits.* MORGAN *goes outside and sits on the back step. Silence, as he looks at the sky and at* ANGUS.

MORGAN	Angus? Bread in the oven.
ANGUS	Uh huh.
MORGAN	Don't forget.
ANGUS	Aww.
MORGAN	How many?
ANGUS	Nineteen thousand, four hundred and forty-four. Total.
MORGAN	That's a lot.

> *Silence.*

ANGUS	Tell it.
MORGAN	Naw.... Not tonight, Angus.
ANGUS	Sure, tonight. You never tell it.
MORGAN	I tell it daily, you just don't.... Alright. Just... listen.

A couple of boys played shinney and went to school and grew up. One drew pictures of a cabin—fine pictures of the inside and the outside—until finally they built the cabin together. Stole nails, played hookey until it was done.

They finished school. One just barely. The other finished easily, but never got his diploma because he wouldn't give back the poetry book. That one almost went off to school, to keep drawing. The other one never would of. He was all set to work for his father, to start in on the farm. And then they both got called up, both went off to Europe. No school for the one, no farm for the other. They managed to stick together.

> MILES *comes into the kitchen to retrieve his pen, and overhears the following.*

They fired their guns straight up in the air, and yelled to each other the louder things got. When it got so loud they couldn't hear, they sang. They had three boots between them.

In England they met two girls, one tall and one taller. The taller one liked the drawer; the tall one, the farmer. They talked, they made plans. The girls talked together, the boys talked together.

The tall girl and the farmer would talk all night. The taller girl and the drawer would walk and talk all night. One girl would talk to the other boy about the boy she liked; so would the other girl to the other boy about the first boy.

Also, they talked in threes. Drawer boy, two tall girls; farmer boy, two tall girls; tall girl and two boys; taller girl and two boys. They talked to themselves, too.

The plans they made were like something the one boy would draw: Inside and out, all the details mixed, and when they were done talking, all four got ready to come home.

One night, in an air raid, the drawer boy was outside. The tall English girls and his friend were together and safe, in the butler's pantry of a large and empty house. They lit candles and made jokes about where the other one might be.

Well, he was down the street, looking at another large house. Probably staring at the wrought iron, or memorizing the slope of the roof. The front door of the house flew off when the shell hit, and the drawer boy watched it come for him.

A doctor took two inches of copper plate out of the boy's head, from the front-door door-knocker. The doctor put in twenty-six millimeters of stainless steel. Before the doctor could close up the wound, the boy's memory escaped.

His hair grew back and the boy's three friends slowly put his memory back, too. One day he woke up and remembered right and left, and up and down. One day he woke up and remembered he loved the taller English girl. They got ready to go home again, talked about their plans again. They showed the drawer boy pictures he made of the house all four would live in, pictures he had made before the front door came. He could not remember making the pictures, but he agreed to the plan: They would come home. There would be a double wedding. There was money enough for one piece of land. The house would be built on a farm they would share, and it would be two houses joined. Two families would be started, life would begin for the four friends.

They came home. There was a double wedding. The drawer boy recited a poem from the stolen book. They bought one piece of land. They started to build the house. They bought a car. They bought an old black car.

ANGUS   Right.

MORGAN   The taller English girl loved to drive, and one day she and the tall English girl went in the old black car to a berry bush the farmer boy had shown them. Coming home, there were two pails of raspberries between them on the seats. They knew what side of the road to be on. They did. An old army transport came over the hill on their side, coming toward them; the transport was passing a horse. The taller English girl turned, turned her side of the old black car into the transport, because she knew they could not miss. Her side of the old car was just ruined. Not a scratch on the tall girl's side. But the tall girl died too.

ANGUS   Right. My Sally. My... Sally. Your?

MORGAN   My Frances. Then the two tall English girls went to a hill, both in the same carriage, pulled by a horse. The hill is the highest point in the county. That's where they are now. And then, it was the two friends again. And the drawer makes bread and adds rows of numbers in his head, and the farmer farms and tends to the place on the hill and keeps their memories safe, like a pail of raspberries between them.

ANGUS   Right. Morgan. I smell bread.

MORGAN   You do? How do you feel? How's your head?

ANGUS   No. I smell bread.

MORGAN   *(jumping up)* Jesus.

           MORGAN *runs into the kitchen to rescue the bread.* MILES *escapes without being seen.*

MORGAN   *(pulling the burnt bread out of oven)* Jesus! Angus! Goddamn it!

ANGUS   Nineteen thousand, four hundred and forty... five.

ACT 1, SCENE 6

           Late that night. MILES *comes into the kitchen. He pulls out his notebook.*

MILES   Two friends built a cabin with nails they stole from.... Two friends grew up together; one was a farmer, one drew pictures. They made plans, they went to school. They went off to war. They shot their guns in the air and sang war songs. They had three boots between them. They met two English girls, one tall and one taller.

ANGUS *enters in his pyjamas. He's searching for something. As* MILES *watches, he goes carefully through the kitchen, beginning again with the blank space on the wall. Eventually, he sees* MILES.

ANGUS   Hey! Who are you??

MILES   My name's Miles. I'm staying with you and Morgan to learn about farming so I can write a play about it.

ANGUS   *(waves)* Okay. Hello, Miles.

ANGUS *sits down at the table. He looks at* MILES.

MILES   Did you come down for something? It's a couple of hours until we have to rotate the crops.

ANGUS   Eh?

MILES   Were you looking for something?

ANGUS   Sure.

MILES   What?

ANGUS   No idea.

MILES   ...Should you go to bed then?

ANGUS   You bet.

ANGUS *gets up, hesitates, then heads outside.* MILES *follows, and watches as* ANGUS *stands, looking at the stars.*

MILES   Angus?

ANGUS   You bet.

MILES   Nice night.

ANGUS   That's right. *(silence)* You organize it into sections. The whole sky. It's just pieces. No bigger than you. Then you count it. *(silence, then* ANGUS *turns to* MILES*)* See?

MILES   Uh huh.

> ANGUS *goes inside. He repeats exactly the same moves from earlier, looking for something.* MILES *watches him for a while.*

MILES   Can I help you find it?

ANGUS   Jeez. I couldn't tell ya. You hungry?

MILES   Not really.

ANGUS   Me neither.

> ANGUS *leaves. After a moment,* MILES *returns to his notebook.*

ACT 1, SCENE 7

> *An afternoon, a couple of days later.* MORGAN *and* ANGUS *enter,* ANGUS *is excited.*

ANGUS   That was exactly right, wasn't it? The tractor? Them two girls were the tires, and the one fella on the other's shoulders, and he was driving the fella and the two girls, because they were the tractor. And telling about the tractor breaking down when the harvest hasta come in, and how you gotta be awake when you go over hills and the like. The fella sitting on top of the fella's shoulders, talking away to us while he's driving the tractor. That was exactly right.

MORGAN   Uh huh.

ANGUS   And that girl who came out and said she was... was....

MORGAN   Alison Lobb.

ANGUS   That's right. D'you know for a long while there I thought she was Alison Lobb? I thought, good Lord, Alison Lobb's lost her senses and gone up there on the stage and was talking to us. It wasn't, you know. That was an actress. Acting.

MORGAN   I know.

ANGUS   *I laughed.* And then... Miles comes out and starts with that story about the two tall English girls, and the war and all, in that funny voice, and all of a sudden I realized—it's you! He's pretending to be you and that's why I knew the story just before he said each word. He told it just the way you do! I remembered all of it as he said it, I could have said it along with him.... Hey! Shit! That other fella! The simple-looking fella he was telling the story to! That was me! The one fella was you and the other one was supposed to be me! Jesus, that was something. That was us.

MORGAN   That was us.

ANGUS   He got us, didn't he? Miles. He got us.

MORGAN   He did.

ANGUS   He did. I'll never forget that. I can't wait until everyone—

MORGAN   Angus? Want a sandwich?

ANGUS   Sure. *(gets sandwich materials out of fridge, starts to make two)* I'll tell yuh, Morgan, that was just... I never seen....

MORGAN   Angus? How many stars you count last night?

ANGUS   Six-hundred and eighteen I never counted before. One thousand and seventy-nine I already did.

MORGAN   Got a new total?

ANGUS   Sure. Twenty-two thousand, seven-hundred and fifty-seven. New total.

MORGAN   Good. What did we do today?

ANGUS   Aaww. We just got back.

MORGAN   From where.

ANGUS   From... town?

MORGAN   What on earth were we doing in town?

ANGUS   Well, Morgan, I don't know. We were... I don't... I'm hungry, though. Sandwich?

MORGAN   Okay.

> MORGAN *sees* MILES *coming into the yard, and goes out to intercept him.*

MILES   What'd you think of the rehearsal? A lot of it's pretty rough, but I thought some of it went—

MORGAN   You get out of here.

MILES   ...I'm sorry?

MORGAN   You heard. Get out. You can't stay here.

MILES   Morgan, hold it. You're upset I used that story and didn't tell you—I wanted that to be a surprise.

MORGAN   It was. You put that in your play and I'll see to it you never put it on.

MILES   Look, if I didn't get the story exactly right, it's because I only heard it once. You can give me the details, we can work on it together. It's important. We're here to get your history and give it back to you.

MORGAN   It ain't—you can't use that. It's private between Angus and me, and I don't want people to hear it.

MILES   Everyone around here must know the story already. I just want to tell it to them in the play, so they can see how important it is.

MORGAN   Just get out of here. You can't stay. You lied.

MILES   What does Angus say about it?

MORGAN   Angus's already forgotten it, thank God. You oughta be ashamed, coming here, stealing....

MILES	Morgan, listen to me. It's the only thing I've got in the show right now. If I cut this scene—which the director loves, by the way—I'm out of the show. Produce or die, remember?

ANGUS *comes outside, sees* MILES.

ANGUS	Hey!!!
MILES	Hello, Angus. My name's—
ANGUS	Miles! We saw you! You were Morgan and that other fella was me! You got us!
MILES	*(pause)* That's right. You remember the play?
MORGAN	You know who that is?
ANGUS	Sure. You're Miles, and you're staying with Morgan and me while you learn about farming and write that play! You were Morgan. You told about us. God! I'll never forget it. Come in and have a sandwich, Miles.
MILES	*(to MORGAN)* Has he ever...?
MORGAN	Never recognized anyone but me.
ANGUS	You were him. You sounded just like Morgan. Come in and have a sandwich.
MORGAN	He has to go now. He's gonna get his things and leave.
ANGUS	Why?
MILES	I don't know, exactly.
ANGUS	Well, that's just silly. You can't go. Just got here.
MORGAN	He's leaving.
ANGUS	Why?
MILES	Because of what I did on stage.
ANGUS	Whatareyuh...?

MILES   Your story. About the two tall English girls.
                Morgan says I can't use it.

ANGUS   Oh. Well. Shit. That's not a story. That's us. You
                have to use that.

>   ANGUS *goes back inside.* MILES *and* MOR-
>   GAN *stare at each other.*

                He has to use that. He's here because he's....
                Miles! Get in here! 'Kinda sandwich you want?

>   MILES *goes inside and sits with* ANGUS.

>   *End of Act One.*

ACT TWO

ACT 2, SCENE 1

The next day. MILES *sits on the ground outdoors, talking to* ANGUS. *There are two piles of gravel beside him: a big pile and a little pile. He takes a stone from the big pile, dunks it in a bucket of soapy water, scrubs it with a vegetable brush, and dries it carefully with a small towel. Then he puts it onto the small pile.*

ANGUS *sits on the back step, listening.*

MILES   ...and I have these two friends. From university. They're funny. They talk alike, and they sort of dress alike, and they're always together. And because I'm sad, my stepfather calls them up and says, "He mopes around wearing black all day, come and visit and cheer him up"—and so they do. Except what my stepfather really wants them to do is spy on me, in case I get it into my head that I want to kill him.

ANGUS   Why would you...?

MILES   Because, like I said, he killed my father and married my mum, and my father told me to. Sort of. His ghost sort of told me to.

ANGUS   Right.

MILES   Their names are Rosencrantz and Guildenstern.

ANGUS   You're kidding.

MILES   I am not.

ANGUS   Hee hee.

MILES   So they show up, and I know right off that they're here to spy on me for my stepfather. So I put on an antic disposition. I pretend to go mad. I threaten them, and call them names, and kick them out. Except you start to wonder—am I acting mad, or am I really going mad? I'm all sad and angry, I keep hearing voices, and I can't decide what to do, so I do nothing, and that makes me even worse. I start treating my girl-friend really badly. I yell at her and call her bad names. I just treat her terribly, until she goes mad for sure and drowns herself in a pond.

ANGUS   Miles. You went mad.

MILES   And then I yell at my mother. And—Angus, you aren't baking, are you?

ANGUS   Who knows. You yelled at your mum?

MILES   And then I kill this nice old guy who talked all the time. I stabbed him through the arras.

ANGUS   The arras. Ouch. Were you mad then? Or just pretending?

MILES   Well, you still weren't sure. You still couldn't tell.

ANGUS   But—could you?

MILES   I.... Yes. I think I was a little mad then. I think stabbing a guy makes you go even more mad.

ANGUS   Oh, I know.

MILES   Anyway, by the time I finish talking to my mum and stabbing the old guy, I decide I have to kill my stepfather.

ANGUS   'Cause of hearing your dad's voice?

MILES   Yes.

ANGUS   But, Miles! What if the voice in your head is just some voice? You can't go killing people because of that.

MILES   That's right....

ANGUS   I mean—Jesus!—what if everybody acted that way?

MILES   I know.

ANGUS	Killing people just 'cause of something they heard in their head once or twice.
MILES	I know.
ANGUS	Everybody did that, there'd be no one left. S'not right.
MILES	You're right. That's what I'm so worried about. That's why I went mad.

MORGAN *comes in from the barn, and speaks to* MILES *as he passes.*

MORGAN	Hurry up. I'll need that gravel by after lunch.
ANGUS	Morgan! Hello.

MORGAN *goes inside.*

ANGUS	That's a tough job you've got.
MILES	Yeah, the actor's life's a difficult one.
ANGUS	No. The.... *(points at what* MILES *is doing)*
MILES	Have you ever done this?
ANGUS	Well, I guess I must of, some time. Tough job. So... what... where... Oh! Your stepfather. Didja kill him?
MILES	Well, not right away. My girlfriend's brother comes home. He's mad at me because she killed herself, so we have a couple of sword fights, everybody takes some drugs sort of by accident, and then everybody dies.
ANGUS	Everybody dies by accident?
MILES	Sort of.
ANGUS	Helluvan accident.
MILES	And then I die too.
ANGUS	I should hope so. Did people clap?

MILES	Oh, yeah. People loved it. The people that saw it. The critics hated it.
ANGUS	Why?
MILES	I don't know. They said I was too Canadian.
ANGUS	Well, that makes sense.

          MORGAN *comes back outside with a dessert fork.*

ANGUS	Morgan. Hello. He went mad.
MORGAN	*(to* MILES*)* Here. Know what this is? This is a short-handled insilage fork. After the gravel's washed, I want you to muck out the cow stalls. Using this. Cows have been eating corn lately, and not all of it gets digested. You use this to retrieve the undigested corn and put it into a bucket. We feed the chickens that fortified corn. You understand me?
MILES	Yes. *(MORGAN exits)* He must think I'm so stupid.
ANGUS	Oh, he does.
MILES	As if I'd go through all the cow crap with this. With a stupid little fork.
ANGUS	It's crazy.
MILES	It sure is.
ANGUS	I'll get you a spoon. Tell me another.
MILES	Let's see. Did one about a family from out around here, called the Donnellys. Bad bunch. They were so nasty to so many people, that one night a mob came and burned down their house.
ANGUS	Jeez. Who made that up? That Shakespeare?
MILES	No, a Canadian wrote it, but it's not made up. It's a true story. It really happened.
ANGUS	Whadda ya mean! It was on stage, wasn't it? It was a play.

MILES	It was a play from a true story. Like the one that we're making up now. It's a play about farmers, but the stories we tell in it are true ones. Like the story I heard Morgan tell you.
ANGUS	The two tall English girls.
MILES	Right.
ANGUS	Tell it.
MILES	I don't think so, Angus.
ANGUS	Go on.
MILES	No, I don't think Morgan would like it.
ANGUS	'Course he would. Why wouldn't he?
MILES	Well, because it's his story. His and yours. And he should tell it to you, not me.
ANGUS	Okay.
MILES	Sorry.
ANGUS	No. *(pause)* What if you pretended you were him. You be Morgan, and I'll pretend I'm Angus, and you tell it that way.
MILES	I can't do that.
ANGUS	Can too.
MILES	No, I can't.
ANGUS	Sure, just pretend you're Morgan sitting there washing rocks, and you think to yourself, "Geez, I'd better tell Angus that there tall-girl story before I do another thing." And then say "Angus," and I'll say "What?," and you say the story of the two English tall-girls now hurry up.
MILES	No, look, I can't. It's Morgan's story to tell. It's not right that I start telling it to you.
ANGUS	Oh. Unless you're up on stage telling everybody, right?

MILES	Uhh. Right.
ANGUS	Oh.
MILES	Right, so....
ANGUS	It'd be okay for me, though? To tell it?
MILES	Of course. Yes. I'd love to hear it.
ANGUS	Okay. I'll pretend to be you pretending to be Morgan telling the story. *(he looks around)* Now, would I be on a stage, or....
MILES	No. You're just sitting on the back step.
ANGUS	Oh. Right. Okay then. *(he contorts himself, raises his voice an octave)* Now I'm you. *(he hunches over, drops his voice two octaves)* And now I'm you being Morgan. Any good?
MILES	Perfect.
ANGUS	Perfect. *(pause)* How's it start?
MILES	*(pulls out his notebook)* Once there were two friends....
ANGUS	Once there were two friends....
	As MILES *leads* ANGUS *through the story,* MILES *falls into his "Morgan" persona, until there are two slightly grotesque "Morgans" telling the story back and forth.*
MILES	Two boys. They played hockey together, they did everything together.
ANGUS	Boys who played hockey. And everything.
MILES	The one boy drew pictures.
ANGUS	The one boy drew pictures. The drawer boy.
MILES	Yes. He drew pictures of a cabin. Inside and out, lots of pictures. Then they built the cabin.

ANGUS	Drawer boy drew a cabin, inside and out. Then they stole nails, and played hookey, and built the cabin.
MILES	And then they went off to war together.
ANGUS	And then they went off to war together.
MILES	They fought together, and hid together, and sang when it was loudest. They had three boots between them.
ANGUS	They fired up in the air together, and hid, and sang together when it got too loud, and... three boots.
MILES	In England they met two girls....
ANGUS	One tall and one taller.
MILES	The taller one liked the drawer.
ANGUS	And the tall one liked Morgan. Liked me.
MILES	The tall girl and the farmer would talk all night; the taller girl and the drawer would walk all night and talk. One girl would talk to the other boy about the boy she liked, so would the other girl to the other boy....
ANGUS	They talked....
MILES	When they were done talking, their plans were as complete as something the boy would draw.
ANGUS	When they were done talking, they had a picture of the next thing they would make together, the four of them. They came home and had a double wedding....
MILES	No, Angus. Next is the air raid. The front door flying. Remember?
ANGUS	Uh huh. But. I don't want to.
MILES	Okay.

ANGUS	They went home. There was a double wedding, he said the stolen poem. They started the house, the two houses joined.
MILES	Right.
ANGUS	Where?
MILES	Where what.
ANGUS	Where's the houses joined and separate?
MILES	I don't know.
ANGUS	He said—you said, "They started to build the house."
MILES	You're right.
ANGUS	Where?
MILES	Let's ask him later.
ANGUS	Okay.
MILES	They bought a car.
ANGUS	They bought a black car. Now, Angus, you say "My Sally."
MILES	My Sally. Your...?
ANGUS	My Frances. Your Sally loved to drive the car, the black car. To where raspberries grew wild. A horse came the other way, and the army headed straight for my Frances, but my Sally—your Sally—Sally....
MILES	She turned her side into the truck, to save her friend, Angus. Your Sally tried to save Frances.
ANGUS	She... yes.
MILES	And now it's the two friends again.
ANGUS	And now it's the.... No. They got taken in a cart to the highest point in the county. Buried there.

MILES   Yes. That's right. And now it's the two friends
               again.

ANGUS   And now it's.... I've never been there. The high-
               est point in the county. Hey.

               He's being led by a memory so faint, he behaves
               as though he's smelling something. ANGUS
               walks inside, drops to his knees, and pulls up a
               floorboard. He pulls out a beat-up metal tube,
               khaki green, about three feet long. He opens the
               tube, pulls out several architectural drawings,
               and spreads them out on the table.

               The houses joined. Together and separate.

               MORGAN *enters.* ANGUS *greets him without*
               looking up.

               Morgan! Hello! The houses joined. They never
               got started. Did they? You said they did. I want
               to go to them.

MORGAN   *(to* MILES*)* How did you find these?

MILES   I didn't.

MORGAN   How did you find these?

ANGUS   You hid them. I saw you. You didn't see me.

MORGAN   You remember that?

ANGUS   I... I guess I do....

MILES   You made these?

ANGUS   The two houses joined up. I drew these. Separate
               and joined. I was the drawer boy.

MORGAN   You did. You were.

ANGUS   I am. I want to see her, Morgan. Take me to
               where they are. Up on that hill. The tallest point.
               (to MILES*)* You should come, too. You did this.
               Let's go right now.

               ANGUS *goes outside.*

MORGAN   No, Angus. You're baking.

ANGUS   Well, just—turn off the damn... whatever that is! I want to go now. My Sally.

MORGAN   (*following* ANGUS *out*) Listen to me. We can't go, Angus. Now, just stop this.

ANGUS   Can too. I have to.

MORGAN   Angus! Make me a sandwich. I'm hungry.

ANGUS   Make you...? Make your own damn sandwich, old fella! I got to.... Damn it! I WANT TO GO!

               MILES *comes outside.*

               I been waiting so long. I never—why'd you not ever take me? That's my Sally. That's my WIFE.

MILES   Angus. I'm sure he must of. You don't remember things, you know.

ANGUS   I want to go to them. I'll remember them now.

MORGAN   I'm hungry. I want to eat something.

ANGUS   I'll cook once we get back. Let's go. Why'd you never take me there before?

MORGAN   No.

ANGUS   Yes.

MORGAN   No.

ANGUS/MILES   (*together*) Yes!

MORGAN   (*to* MILES) I beg your pardon?

MILES   Well, I mean, he seems to want to go. I just thought—

MORGAN   Would you excuse us, please? Wait inside.

MILES   Sure.

ANGUS   He'll come too!

MILES	Yes, but, I'm just going to go inside for a while.

MILES *goes inside.*

ANGUS	I'll get the truck—or, you should get the truck, you know where we're going. Plus, do I know how to drive?
MORGAN	Angus, I'm tired. I want my lunch. There's so much I need to do this afternoon.
ANGUS	Not more important than this! There's a picture of the place in my head—the tallest spot—I want to go and match it. Now.
MORGAN	Feed came this morning. Usual amount, and I wrote Wally a cheque. Can we cover it?
ANGUS	Leaves forty-four dollars and sixteen cents. Dairy give us ninety-one twenty-one in the next three days, we can cover the loan and have six-teen-oh-eight to spare—now, let's go.
MORGAN	Angus. No. We aren't going.
ANGUS	*(after a pause)* You eat lunch first. *Then.*
MORGAN	No. Not then.
ANGUS	Yes then. Go now and quick—there's some, there's some... something for a sandwich in the... thing. Quick. Go. I'll wait out here.
MORGAN	Listen to me.
ANGUS	You go! I'll wait patiently for you to come out, and we'll go see—
MORGAN	Listen.
ANGUS	—SEE MY SALLY.

ANGUS *holds his head, has to sit.*

MORGAN	Angus, are you—
ANGUS	GO IN! Go in and come out.

> MORGAN *goes inside. He starts to make a sandwich.*

MILES I believe he will remember this time, if you take him.

MORGAN I'm not taking him.

ANGUS Morgan. Done yet?

MILES But why?

ANGUS Morgan.

MORGAN That's between him and me.

MILES Fine, I don't want to interfere—

ANGUS Morgan! Time's up!

MILES —but he's better now, he seems better. Since rehearsal. He's remembering things. And he wants to go.

MORGAN I told him no, and I'm telling you no.

ANGUS *(holding his head)* Aw, God. Moorgan!

> *Silence while* MORGAN *finishes making the sandwich, sits, and begins to eat.*

Morgan! Let's go! Morgan! Mooorgan! You got to drive!

> ANGUS *is in more and more pain.*

Moooorgan!!

MILES Morgan, Jesus....

MORGAN How's the gravel coming?

MILES I'll take him myself. Just tell me where it is.

ANGUS Mooorgan! Get the... truck!

MORGAN You got too much to do. Gravel and then the muckin' out.

ANGUS	Aaaaahhh. Morgan! Morgan.
MILES	This is, just, cruel.
ANGUS	*(suddenly no longer in pain)* Morgan! Get the jeep!
MILES	Morgan, for God's sake.
ANGUS	Get a, we need a jeep! Don't tell anyone! Morgan!
MORGAN	*(goes to the door)* Angus! Come indoors.
ANGUS	Morgan! Hello! We need a ride. We can't tell anyone. We got to go.
MORGAN	Come inside.

They go inside.

ANGUS	What did you do to get us passes? Sergeant says don't tell anyone, and be back by oh-six-hundred. Jesus, Morgan! Miles. You can't come.
MORGAN	Angus, listen—
ANGUS	Sally will just—let's go now. Surprise them.
MORGAN	Angus? You need to go upstairs. To bed, now.
ANGUS	To hell with that! They're waiting for us. Did you call? Did you?
MORGAN	I.... Yes. I did.
ANGUS	I knew it! Jesus, you did. Goddamn it! You set it all up.
MORGAN	That's right. I did.
ANGUS	Yuh clever bastard! Let's go. Miles. You can't go. The girls are waiting, but we got just the two passes. Morgan set it up.
MILES	Angus. I'm sorry. I don't understand you.
MORGAN	This happened.
MILES	What?

MORGAN	I got leave for the two of us overnight. It was his birthday. It was a surprise.
MILES	He remembers!
MORGAN	This is your fault.
ANGUS	You've got to lend me some shoes, mine are still wet from the ditch. Sergeant says we have to... we have to be back... *(his headache resumes)* Morgan? It's too bright.
MORGAN	Let's go, Angus. Upstairs.
ANGUS	No! She's waiting with... to give me... cufflinks.
MORGAN	You can't go like that. Can you.
ANGUS	No. Not like this.
MORGAN	Let's go up and get your uniform on.
ANGUS	Okay.
MORGAN	Get you that shoe.
ANGUS	Let's... hurry. *(looks at MILES)* Hey. Who're you?
MORGAN	That's the man who did this to you.

MORGAN *leads* ANGUS *upstairs.*

ACT 2, SCENE 2

Late that night. ANGUS *walks into the kitchen. As in Act One, he's looking for something. He comes across the architectural drawings, and stares at them for a while.*

ANGUS	"God with honour hang your head, Groom, and grace you bride, your bed, With lissome scions, sweet scions, Out of hallowed bodies bred.

"Each be other's comfort kind:
Deep, deeper than divined—"

He looks up.

Morgan?

He gets no response, and goes back to the blue-prints.

I want to....

He looks out the door, then looks back toward the stairs.

I'll go. I'll go now.

He goes out the back door and off into the night. After a moment, MORGAN comes into the kitchen.

MORGAN   Angus? *(sees the open back door and goes out)* Angus? Angus!!

He walks off. MILES comes into the kitchen.

MILES   Morgan? What is it.

MORGAN comes back into the house. He pulls on his boots, puts on a jacket.

MORGAN   He's gone.

MILES   Oh, no. He went to the graveyard. I'll go....

MORGAN   You stay here.

MILES   Look—I'm "the man who did this." I want to help.

MORGAN   *You stay here.*

MORGAN exits.

ACT 2, SCENE 3

Dawn. MILES *is sitting in the kitchen, waiting impatiently. He gets up and goes outside. He sees the two piles of rocks left over from the day before; picks up a rock, dunks it in the pail of water, dries it with the cloth, and sets it on the small pile. He does this again, distractedly. Then he looks around, surreptitiously; picks up the bucket of water, dumps the water on the larger pile of rocks, pats the pile dry a couple of times, and then pushes the big pile and the little pile together.*

MORGAN *enters.*

MORGAN	Anybody call?
MILES	No. Any luck?
MORGAN	No.

MORGAN goes inside. He doesn't know what to do with himself. He makes a sandwich. MILES *goes in.*

ANGUS *walks through the yard unseen, his arm bleeding, and then goes off again.*

MILES	He'll turn up. *(pause)* Finished the gravel.
MORGAN	Huh? Oh. Goes in the culvert.
MILES	Sure. Is the culvert that shed thing out behind the barn?
MORGAN	No, it's... never mind. I'll do it. *(goes to the phone and dials)* Tom? Morgan. Any sign of him? Okay. Thanks. *(hangs up)*
MILES	What about the graveyard?
MORGAN	What about it.
MILES	Did you look there.
MORGAN	No.
MILES	But that's where he wanted to go.

MORGAN	I'm gonna say this once, as nice as I can under the circumstances: You are not being helpful.
MILES	Fine. I'm sorry. Tell me how I can help.
MORGAN	Go to the henhouse. Shuffle the eggs.
MILES	Morgan—
MORGAN	Take the eggs out from underneath each chicken, put them under a different chicken.
MILES	Look—
MORGAN	That way, they don't raise a fuss when we take their eggs away for good.
MILES	Stop it.
MORGAN	And no chicken has to suffer.
MILES	Tell me why you wouldn't take him to the graveyard. Why you won't look for him there now.
MORGAN	Why? Your play not long enough yet?
MILES	Because I did something to Angus, and I hurt you, and I don't know how I did that. And I want to fix it.
MORGAN	I'll fix it.
MILES	Tremendous. Fix it. Go to the graveyard and get him. Go now.
MORGAN	Cows need to be milked.
MILES	I'll milk the goddamn cows!
MORGAN	Oh, you will, will you? Think you could figure out the milking machine on your own?
MILES	Yes. I do.

ANGUS *walks into the yard again.*

MORGAN	You can't recognize the useful end of a shovel. You go out there, the barn'll fall over.

MILES	I'll do it. Go. Or I'll call the cops and send them up there for him.
MORGAN	You'll what?
MILES	And I'll tell them that you knew he was out wandering around, and you wouldn't go to get him.
MORGAN	You're gonna call the police?
MILES	I.... No, of course not. I just—I don't understand it. We both know where he is, we both know why he went there, and I can't figure out why you won't—
MORGAN	Stop trying.
MILES	—why you won't go and get him. He could be hurt, he could be God knows what. Jesus, Morgan. Don't you care?
MORGAN	You watch your step, young man.
MILES	Tell me why you won't go. Tell me why you're just standing there.
MORGAN	(*tosses his truck keys to MILES*) You go.
MILES	Okay. Thank you. I will.

> MILES *turns to go. But before he gets outside, he stops suddenly and turns to* MORGAN.

MILES	It's not true. What you tell him isn't true. That's why you won't go. Isn't it.
MORGAN	You get out of here

> MILES *leaves; he sees* ANGUS.

MILES	Morgan!
ANGUS	(*to MILES*) What did you...?

> MORGAN *comes outdoors.*

MORGAN	Angus! Are you alright? What happened to you? Where did you get to?
ANGUS	(*to MORGAN*) What did he mean?

MORGAN	(*to MILES*) You leave us alone?
MILES	Sure.
	He goes.
MORGAN	Angus? You alright? Come inside.
	ANGUS goes in.
MORGAN	Sit down. Lemme look at that arm. How did this happen?
ANGUS	What did...he mean?
MORGAN	You hungry? Want a sandwich?
ANGUS	No, I heard, I... what --
MORGAN	Jesus, Angus. You haven't walked off for some time. Once I found you up in the mow, looked all day, and your one leg had gone through a hole and you were just stuck there. You didn't care. Looking off, like you were waiting for a train or something. Do you know, I pulled you out, carried you down and it took you till the next day to come back to yourself. You scared me. What were you thinking about? You'd do it when we were kids. I'd find you up on a tree somewhere, you'd be staring off, I'd be yelling"Angus, Angus", and you'd come back to yourself, climb back down, ask what day it was. It was funny when we were kids.
	I'm gonna make you something to eat and I want you to eat it.
ANGUS	No. Please.
	MORGAN goes to the fridge, starts sandwich-making. He stops and then goes to the sink, gets a spoonful of water, and gives it to ANGUS.
ANGUS	Okay, but. I don't...
MORGAN	*Hush now.*
	MORGAN then goes back to the sandwich. Angus looks down at the blueprints.

ANGUS	The houses joined. Together and separate.
MORGAN	Yes.
ANGUS	I drew these.
MORGAN	Yes.
ANGUS	Don't remember doing that. Remember him hiding them, though. I saw him hide them.
MORGAN	Saw who?
ANGUS	Him. He didn't see me.
MORGAN	Angus. Look at me. Who am I?
ANGUS	You're the man who did this to me.
MORGAN	What's my name.
ANGUS	Don't you know?
MORGAN	Look at me.
ANGUS	You played the farmer boy. You got us.
MORGAN	No Angus.
ANGUS	Sure.
MORGAN	No, Angus. Please. Tell me who I am.
ANGUS	Why should I?
MORGAN	I want to know if you're okay.
ANGUS	I don't care. I was in the dark, walking, and I got stopped. I heard a voice. It was a ghost, it stopped me, it warned me against you.
MORGAN	What?
ANGUS	It told me what you did. It told me I should be afraid of you. It said: HE KILLED YOUR FATHER. HE MARRIED YOUR MUM.
MORGAN	Angus, you're scaring me.

ANGUS   (*a pause. He finally looks at MORGAN*) Good. Okay. I was just pretending. I was pretending I was mad. There was no voice. It was my antic disposition. Morgan. I'm scared. Listen, I was out there, and I heard. He said, Miles said "It's not true. What you tell him isn't true. I heard.

MORGAN   You did.

ANGUS   Yes. Miles said "It's not true. What you tell him isn't true." did he mean me?

MORGAN   Yes.

ANGUS   Oh. What did he mean ?

MORGAN   He means I lied. I lied to you.

ANGUS   Is that true?

MORGAN   Yes.

ANGUS   Oh. Okay. You lied. You're a bastard. God. Look. The houses joined. Where's Miles. I want him to tell it.

MORGAN   Not now.

ANGUS   Yes. now. I want—Miles to. He, what did he do? Oh God, Morgan.

MORGAN   What's wrong?

ANGUS   What'd he do to me? I have, in my head.....

MORGAN   What. Tell me.

ANGUS   Just everything. Just... everything. It came all night. Listen: I'm a boy, and I have a cough and a nosebleed on my shirt. On my short pants. I remembered that. Then, another time, I'm writing a test, and the smell of you sittin' beside me, smell of you failing it. I remember France, that boy running away. You would not shoot the boy running away. Sally, the first sigh of her from behind in that church. Oh, God, oh no, I remember that. Her hair, my finger trapped in the pages of the hymn book. And, then, I got hurt—God, the noise, I'm lying on the ground.... I remember

when my head didn't hurt, I think. I remember
the double wedding.

MORGAN   You remember the double wedding?

ANGUS   I do. I stood up, I said: "God with honour hang
your head, groom—"

MORGAN   You remember getting hurt?

ANGUS   I do. I remember the door flying. At me. The
three of you safe, and me on my way to you,
and I got stopped by the architecture.

MORGAN   No, that's—oh, Jesus.

ANGUS   I remember everything.

MORGAN   No, you don't.

ANGUS   Yes. Yes, I do! It came all night. I walked. I was
looking for them.

MORGAN   You remember the story. What he said on stage.

ANGUS   No. I remember *it*.

MORGAN   What was in your hand?

ANGUS   My hand?

MORGAN   What were you carrying?

ANGUS   Nothing. I don't think....

MORGAN   What you just told me is what I've told you all
these years. That's our story. What you had in
your hand was a bottle of cheap brandy, given to
me in a card game. I sent you to fetch it.
Remember? *We laughed*, and I made you get it.
You were safe, and I sent you out—you under-
stand? Angus? I did that. I did that to you. That's
the first thing.

ANGUS   That's the first thing? See. You're a bastard. What
do I remember?

MORGAN   You remember the story.

ANGUS   Aw, God.

MORGAN   Angus. What'd I get for that car?

ANGUS   Car?

MORGAN   The black car.

ANGUS   It got wrecked. The army truck.

MORGAN   Did it? If you can remember, then remember.

ANGUS   Don't.

MORGAN   What'd I get for that car.

ANGUS   It got wrecked, my Sally was driving, and she turned it into the truck—

MORGAN   No. It's a number.

ANGUS   I don't want to. I want him—I want the story.

MORGAN   How much'd I get for that car?

ANGUS   Hundred and ten dollars.

MORGAN   That's right.

ANGUS   Hundred and ten dollars. Oh. From Doug Hamm. It didn't crash.

MORGAN   That's right. We sold it. You do remember.

ANGUS   No, I don't.

MORGAN   Angus, listen—

ANGUS   No. It's not true. "What you tell him isn't true." I heard.

MORGAN   It is true.

ANGUS   Where's Miles? Hey! Miles! Get in here!

MORGAN   No, Angus, wait.

ANGUS   I want him. Miles!

MILES *runs on.*

> *(to* MILES*)* You said, "What you tell him isn't true." He said, "I lied." He lied. He's a bastard. Now he says something... else. You have to tell it.

MILES   Morgan'll tell you.

ANGUS   No, he won't. He's a bastard. You will. You know.

MILES   Angus. Do you know what I am? I'm an actor. I play at things. I was playing Morgan when you saw me. But he's here. He's right there, and he can tell you.

ANGUS   He lied. I remember you.

MILES   Listen to me. Do you know what I did? Just now? I was out in the barn, pretending to be a farmer. All those cows were in agony, they were all begging to be milked, and do you know what I did? I broke the milking machine. I hooked it up to Daisy and switched it on, and she groaned, and then the whole thing stopped. I broke it. I don't know what I'm doing, Angus. Let Morgan tell you.

ANGUS   You broke the milking machine?

MILES   Yes.

ANGUS   Oh boy.

MORGAN   *(simultaneous with the above)* Aw, Jesus.

MILES   Sorry. You were right. But you don't need to rush out there. Daisy's okay. They're all okay. I milked them by hand.

MORGAN   You milked nine cows by hand?

MILES   Well, a little bit each. Just to take the pressure off. I was standing there amid all these weeping cows. I had to do something. I just sat down, grabbed hold, and got the hang of it pretty fast. I just went from cow to cow, one after another— grab, milk, grab, milk, grab, milk, grab, milk.... Suddenly, I looked up, and it was done.

MORGAN   What'd you do when the bucket got full?

MILES   You're supposed to use a bucket?

ANGUS	Oh boy.
MILES	I've got to go. I've got rehearsal....
ANGUS	No! Tell it.
MORGAN	I am. I will.
ANGUS	No. Him.
MILES	Angus, no.
ANGUS	Okay. Both of you. Tell it.
MORGAN	I will, but not with him here.
ANGUS	Yes, with him here. I'm scared. You're scaring me, yuh bastard. From the start. Both of you.
MORGAN	Angus, don't—
ANGUS	BOTH OF YOU. Please. So I can match them. Find me in them. I'm starved to know.
MORGAN	Alright.
ANGUS	Right. Go. You start.
MILES	Okay.
ANGUS	But, as him.
MILES	Right.
ANGUS	Like you did, on the... thing.
MILES	I got it. *(as MORGAN)* A couple of boys played shinney, and went to school, and grew up.
ANGUS	Now you.
MORGAN	They built—
ANGUS	But, as you.
MORGAN	...We built a cabin together. You dreamed it up, I did all the work.
MILES	Stole nails, and played hookey, and built a cabin. From the drawer boy's pictures.

MORGAN	You were about to go to university. I talked you out of it. The war started, and I talked you into volunteering with me. It was going to be an adventure. We were so excited. No. I was excited, and you were—you were my friend. We joined up. As soon as we got over there, we were at an air field, and we saw something. A stupid accident during training. Do you remember?
ANGUS	I....
MORGAN	We watched three men burn to death. We couldn't help. It was awful. And then the only thing we did was survive. We never volunteered for anything, we hid when things got bad. We'd use up ammunition by shooting straight up.
MILES	Then, they met two girls. One tall, and one taller. The taller one liked the drawer, the tall one, the farmer.
MORGAN	They agreed to marry us. They agreed to come home with us. They were friends, like we were friends. The four of us were together as much as possible. We would spend whole nights talking, the four of us. You and Sally would take long walks and count the stars. She taught you how. She knew the names of stars, and how to cut the sky up into manageable pieces for counting. It was the first thing she gave you.
MILES	They made plans. By the time they were done talking, they had a picture of what they would do, like something the one boy would draw.
MORGAN	All we had to do was wait out our tour. All we had to do was keep hiding. Then, one night in an air raid, I sent you out, to get a bottle of brandy I left in Sally's car. We decided we wanted a drink. We were all together, we felt indestructible, because of—because of each other. Like the war was just a dream or something. You took a long time to come back. We made jokes about where you might be. I said to Sally, "He's found someone else."
MILES	The drawer boy was standing down the street, looking at a large house.

MORGAN   You were running like hell down the street, trying to get back. Jesus. You were laughing.

MILES   The front door of the house flew off when the shell hit, and the drawer boy watched it come for him.

MORGAN   A piece of shrapnel caught you from behind. I watched you get carried through the air. You flew right at me. You nearly died. But you didn't. You woke up. But your memory was... gone.

          We came home. They came with us. There was no double wedding. Sally wanted to wait until you were better.

ANGUS   But—the stolen poem....

MORGAN   You never said it. You've been waiting to say it.

          We bought this land. We lived here, in the house that came with the land, English girls in one room, us in the other. The house you designed was never started. We tacked the plans up over there (*indicates the spot where* ANGUS *looks first when he's searching*), so that we could see every day what we intended to do. Eventually, they became just a... reminder. So, one day when you were asleep, when I thought you were asleep, I took them down and I hid them. We did buy an old car, so they could go into town. They were lonely. The car didn't help much.

          Sally looked after you. She stayed by you all the time, every minute. She watched you wander off, she'd follow behind, hiding behind trees so you wouldn't see. You'd get lost, she'd be there, and she'd bring you back home. She'd clean you. She'd feed you. She gave you medicine from a spoon.

          You kept having headaches. They made you different, Angus. They made you mean. Because she was always there, you'd get mean at Sally.

ANGUS   (*to himself*) At Sally.

MORGAN   One day, she was very tired. It was hot, hot like they'd never felt at home. You had another headache. Sally was cooking, baking bread, and you came up to her, and without saying a thing, you hit her. She cried and cried; she wasn't hurt much, but she was tired. You looked at her, and then you had to ask me who that crying girl was. And it was then that Sally decided to leave.

ANGUS   Your Frances...?

MORGAN They were friends. They were here alone.

The day they went, they called a taxi from town. You were asleep. I was here *(in the kitchen doorway)*, I couldn't move. The taxi came, and I went to help Frances with her suitcase, and she said, "This is the worst thing I could do to you. Don't you dare help me do it." She dragged it outside and snarled at the taxi driver when he tried to help her. She was crying from the effort of it. The suitcase made a little trench across the driveway where she dragged it. They got in the taxi. They left. I've not heard a word from her in all this time.

When you woke up—

ANGUS   No.

MORGAN When you woke up, you knew something was wrong. You went into their room. Looked in the closet, looked under the bed. Tore the room apart. You didn't know what you were looking for. You went through all the rooms, looking, and when you had searched the whole house, you started again. You tore through the house, faster and faster—you wouldn't stop, Angus, and you couldn't say what you were looking for. Finally, when you were racing up the stairs to start over again, I tackled you. I hauled you down, and we sat on the stairs, and I told you the lie. I told you the story of the black car crashing for the first time. I told it again, and you stopped crying. I told it again, and you fell asleep. I kept telling it 'cause it made you feel better. Goddamn it, it made me feel better.

     Pause.

ANGUS   I hit my Sally, and you lost your....

MORGAN Yes.

ANGUS   That's what I did to you. God, you must hate me.

MORGAN   I guess I did, Angus.

ANGUS   So. That's me. I'm scared I'll forget *that* now.

MORGAN   We'll tell it to each other. Daily.

ANGUS   Okay. Thank you.

MORGAN   We'll fill it all in. If you can remember, we'll do that.

ANGUS   Even if I don't. Let's do that.

MORGAN   Okay.

ANGUS   *(to* MILES*)* He was right. You are the man who did this to me.

MILES   I'm late. I should go.

ANGUS   Go?

MILES   I have to go to work. To rehearse.

ANGUS   Yes. You're making a....

MILES   That's right.

ANGUS   Miles? That was just a story.

MILES   I know.

ANGUS   No, I mean—you can use it if you want.

MILES   Thanks. But—thanks.

            MILES *takes his notebook out of his pocket,
            hands it to* MORGAN, *then leaves.*

ANGUS   That was Miles. He's here staying with you and me while he puts on a play about farming. You told him awful stories.

MORGAN   Yes.

ANGUS   And you're Morgan.

MORGAN   Yes. And you're Angus.

ANGUS   You carried me—and all that—around all this time? Since the taxi went?

MORGAN   Yes.

ANGUS   Must be tired. I'll make you a sandwich. Or—here—someone made this one already.

MORGAN   Thanks. I'd better go outside and see what he's done to the barn.

      MORGAN *exits.*

ANGUS   "God with honour hang your head,
Groom, and grace you bride, your bed
With lissome scions, sweet scions,
Out of hallowed bodies bred.

"Each be other's comfort kind:
Deep, deeper than divined..."

MORGAN   *(from off)* Angus! The bulk cooler's full of milk! He used the milking machine after all. He was—he was lying to us, the silly bugger!

ANGUS   "...Divine charity, dear charity,
Fast you ever, fast bind.

"Then let the march tread our ears:
I to him turn with tears
Who to wedlock, his wonder wedlock,
Deals triumph and immortal years."

      As the lights fade, ANGUS *takes the drawings and holds them up where they used to live.*

      The End.